MARRIAGE CHALLENGES

for Her

*One Year of Weekly Suggestions to Love Your
Husband More Effectively and Transform Your Marriage*

MANDY SHROCK

Library of Congress Control Number: 2022918909
ISBN: 978-1-958477-07-6 (Paperback)
ISBN: 978-1-958477-08-3 (Digital Online)

Cover and Interior Design by KUHN Design Group | kuhndesigngroup.com

First printing edition 2022.

Published by In Abundance, LLC

info@marriageinabundance.com

CONTENTS

FOREWORD

This book of suggested marriage challenges is just "one part of a whole" for Marriage In Abundance's approach to a better marriage. Our goal at Marriage In Abundance is to help couples discover just how deep and meaningful their marriage relationship can be. For best results, this book, along with *Marriage Challenges for Him,* is to be used in conjunction with *Marriage In Abundance's Date Plans for Married Couples* and *Devotions for Married Couples.* To find access to the full program, visit www.marriageinabundance.com.

Here's an overview of what you'll find through Marriage In Abundance:

- **Date Plans for Married Couples**—weekly date plans for fostering creative, engaging, quality time together.

- **Couples' Devotions**—weekly studies to deepen your spiritual connection with God and each other.

- **Marriage Challenges**—weekly suggestions for showing love to one another more effectively, plus monthly suggestions for eliminating unhealthy styles of conflict resolution. As our schedules become over-loaded, marital connection takes a backseat. The marriage challenges bring intentionality to meeting one another's needs and desires and spicing up the romance.

INTRODUCTION

WHAT ARE MARRIAGE CHALLENGES?

Sometimes, in trying to meet all of life's demands, connection with our spouse takes a backseat. We fall into a routine that feels more like roommates than lovers. Unless we're intentional about keeping the connection and romance alive, the spark will dwindle. Completing the weekly marriage challenges is a way to be intentional about expressing your love for your husband amid the hustle and bustle and keeping the romance alive.

We all have different needs, desires, and ways we feel loved. Maybe hugs don't mean much to you, but a love note does. Maybe sweet-nothings feel meaningless compared to a thoughtful gesture. Typically, when we express love to one another, we do so in a way we understand it, not the way someone else understands it. In trying to make our husband feel loved, we sometimes "miss the mark." Since marriage challenges touch on every avenue of showing love, if you follow our suggestions, you're sure to express love in a way your husband understands. You may even discover a new way he feels love that neither of you knew before!

In addition to the weekly challenges, which are fun ways to show affection, the once-a-month habit reformation challenges will transform your approach to conflict resolution. If you only add fun to the marriage, but don't eliminate the unhealthy habits—such as yelling, interrupting, manipulating, and name-calling—you won't experience as much growth in the marriage. As old habits die hard, you will have one month to focus on better conflict resolution before moving on to another challenge.

MARRIAGE CHALLENGE INSTRUCTIONS

Separate or Together: Most of the challenges are to be done for each other separately. For example, one week you might be challenged to initiate sex, while your husband is challenged to show gratitude for the little things you do in your day. However, sometimes the challenges are to be done together. For example, be intentional about kissing every day that week. In this case, the challenge will say "together," and you can discuss and complete that challenge together. If it doesn't say "together," don't discuss your challenge, just do it.

No Peeping: It is important to keep your challenges in a place your spouse won't be peeping. We don't recommend spouses hide *anything* from each other *ever*—except for the marriage challenges. If your husband sees your challenge and you have not done it, this sets him up for disappointment and will do more harm than good. If you happen to see his challenge lying around, no snooping! Keep your mind focused on your own challenge.

Romance During Everyday Routine: The challenges can be done at any point that is convenient for you that week. However, if you are also participating in the date plans, the challenges are not meant to be done at the same time as the date. The purpose of the marriage challenges is to add intention and romance into your everyday routines, not just on your date together.

A Way to Remember: Part of the problem in keeping the romance alive in a marriage is that you aren't thinking about romance in your everyday lives. It happens to everyone. When you were dating, you were infatuated—smitten—and spent more time thinking about ways you could express love to him. But after you sealed the deal and fell into busyness, you no longer put as much thought into romance. Remembering to pick up this book each week may prove to be just as difficult. So, we suggest setting a couple alarms on your phone—one alarm to remind yourself to pick up your book and look at your challenge for the week, and a second alarm for a time you can complete your challenge that week.

Explicit Content: Considering the marriage challenge's intent is to reignite the romance, some of the challenges, or "assignments," are sexual in nature. Therefore, it is not recommended to keep your marriage challenge books in a place easily accessible to your children.

If any of the sexual marriage challenges cause friction, or trigger a negative emotional response, skip that challenge, and prayerfully consider whether there's a deeper issue that needs addressed in counseling.

Stretch and Grow: You may not feel like doing some challenges—not because it triggers a negative emotion, but because it's just not "your thing." For example, maybe you're not into dancing but your challenge is to squeeze in a slow dance after dinner on your living room floor. If you don't do your challenge simply because that's not "your thing," you are limiting growth and denying your spouse full enjoyment of you. Comfort zones are confining. You won't grow if you're not willing to stretch.

Fifth Week: There are four challenges each month. Since there is a fifth week every three months, to stay in the habit, we suggest going back and doing one you missed or doing your favorite again.

Stay Positive: When your spouse does, or says, something nice, you may think, *I bet that was his challenge this week. He only did that because he was told to do it.* Another way to look at it is, *I'm so glad my husband wants to show me love and is giving this a try!*

Make It a Lifestyle: Although the intent is for you to focus on completing one challenge per week, our hope is that, as you begin putting them into practice, these expressions of love become a part of your marriage lifestyle.

JANUARY

(Together) What have you been arguing about lately? Take a break from discussing that topic for a week. When it comes to mind, simply pray over it. Discuss it next week, only after having covered it in prayer.

(Together) In the midst of a stressful moment, hug each other and focus on your breaths. Don't end the hug until your breaths are in sync.

Buy him a luxury man's product that he typically wouldn't buy for himself. Ideas: good quality razor, beard oil, cologne, gloves, repair cream for hands, good quality socks.

Thank him for providing for your needs. Be specific about the ways he provides for you.

Tease him with touches. Ideas: gently stroke his inner thighs, kiss his neck and earlobes, run your foot up his leg, turn on music and dance with him while engaging him in a lot more body contact than typical dancing.

FEBRUARY

Practice forgiving your husband quickly. Don't wait for an apology. Make peace priority in the relationship over being "right."

Have a hot cocoa ready for him
when he comes in from the cold.

Throw out that old t-shirt you wear to bed. Wear comfortable, but visually appealing, pajamas.

Pray this prayer inspired by the prayer of Jabez, found in 1 Chronicles 4:10, directly over him each day this week. Set an alarm to remind yourself.

God, bless [hubby's name]. Enlarge his territory [give him success in his career and family life—be specific]! Let your hand be with him and keep him from harm so he will be free from pain.

Tell him, at the end of the week, what specifically you prayed over him.

A man feels rejected and inadequate when his wife turns him down. The next time he initiates intimacy, but you're exhausted or really *do* have a headache, give him a date and time he can expect you. This tells him it's not a rejection of him, but of the inconvenient timing.

MARCH

Don't bash your husband to your friends and family. If you need relationship advice, talk only with a trusted mentor while protecting and honoring his reputation among your family and friends.

(Together) Look into each other's eyes without saying anything for five minutes. What's the point? A scientific study suggested just two minutes of eye gazing increased mutual attraction and passion significantly. Try it to deepen your marital bond. Extra credit: Eye gaze for ten to twenty minutes!

Kiss him goodbye.
Integrate a little butt-
grabbing and ear nibbling.

Let him sleep in one day
this week while you make
him a special breakfast.

Take a step in the opposite direction of total self-sufficiency. Ask him for help with something. Then thank him for his help. (Men feel pride in providing for their woman's needs.)

APRIL

When your husband is doing something that upsets you try "I Statements" instead of "You Statements." "I Statements" put the focus on your feelings instead of placing blame on him. This lowers his defenses and improves communication. For example, instead of, "You never help me around the house," replace it with, "I feel overwhelmed by the housework piling up. I would really appreciate help." Instead of, "You keep interrupting me!" try, "I feel like my thoughts aren't important when I don't get to finish expressing what's in my head."

(Together) Try a new breathing technique while making love. During the act, focus on your breaths. As you breathe in, arch your back while imagining your pelvic floor moving away from you. As you breathe out, think about it returning to you. This exercise heightens your awareness to that area and increases sensation.

Text or tell him,
"I'm proud to be your wife
because [fill in the blank]."

When passing by him in close quarters, brush against him suggestively.

Frame his favorite photo of the
two of you together. Write a
brief love memo on it. Then,
place it in his briefcase, office, or
another place he'll see it daily.

MAY

Admit an area you've been wrong. This may make us *feel* small, but in truth, it is admirable, displays maturity, and is one giant step forward for a relationship.

Jump in the shower with him
and shower him with attention.

Feel his biceps. Yeah, this is weird, but trust me: he *really* wants you to notice.

Think of a time he made you happy. (Not something he's *not* doing or that you wish he would. Instead, think of something he, actually, said or did.) Text or tell him out of the blue, "I loved it when you…"

What has he most been
complaining about lately?
Research remedies for him.

JUNE

When our happiness requires
something from someone else,
that is unhealthy. Remove that
expectation from your husband.
If needed, seek outside help for
depression or other issues.

(Together) Develop a new routine to spend ten to fifteen minutes each day communicating about your day. Ideas: Go for a walk after dinner or sit on the patio after the kids go to bed.

Plan an evening of intimacy. Give him a tease of what's to come before he leaves for work the morning of the planned rendezvous. He'll be anticipating it all day!

Do a job for him that he normally does, like taking out the trash, mowing, sweeping out the garage, or cleaning the cars.

Massage his head.

JULY

Don't name-call or use words
that attack your husband's
character. Remember the goal
is to resolve conflict and act as
a team, not to cause your hubby
to feel defeated as a person.

(Together) Add a little romance into each day with kiss variety!

Sunday: While engaged in a sensuous kiss, suck your spouse's bottom lip.

Monday: Nibble your spouse's earlobe.

Tuesday: Kiss while one of you is upside down. (Since we're not superheroes, one of you can lie on the couch or bed.)

Wednesday: Put on lipstick and leave your mark.

Thursday: Give your spouse's neck some sensational attention.

Friday: Kiss for at least ten minutes while your lips and tongue explore and rediscover each other's mouth.

Saturday: Kiss while thinking tender, loving thoughts about your spouse. The difference can be surprising!

Ask him to join you in baking a dessert. "Accidentally," get food on him—on multiple body parts. Insist you must lick it off. Extra credit: Move it to the bedroom.

Text him—or place a sticky note somewhere visible—Scripture to encourage him in the specific trial he is currently going through.

Whisper something in your hubby's ear you know will turn him on.

Ideas: *I'm craving you. I love the way you feel inside me. I'm not wearing anything under my clothes. You are so hot.*

AUGUST

Don't interrupt. Allow your husband to finish his thoughts before speaking.

Speak Proverbs 31 over yourself every day this week, substituting your own name in place of "she."

See Appendix.

The next time you're out in public together, discretely give him a little touching/teasing.

Take his picture when he's
engaged in something he
enjoys. Make it the background
of your phone or computer.

Sit on his lap, or as "up close and personal" as you comfortably can. (Extra credit: Straddle him.)

Run your hands through his hair, along his neck, and across his chest.

SEPTEMBER

Stay on the same team in parenting. If one of you makes a rule, the other supports it. If you disagree with your spouse's parenting decision, talk about it in private— not in front of the kids—and then present your agreed-upon decision to the kids, together as a husband-wife team. Not only is it important for kids to have consistency, but for a family to be healthy, the marriage relationship needs to be stronger than the parent-child relationship.

(Together) Worship together
and lift your marriage up to
God while worshipping. This
can be through either a personal
experience in your home or during
the church worship service.

Point out to your husband
what he's doing well.

Make him feel special, wait on him, and treat him like a king for whatever chunk of time you can carve out this week—a half hour, a few hours, a day. Don't forget to bring your best attitude. Ideas: make his favorite food, shower him with affection, ask him what would make him the happiest man on the planet and then deliver.

Deliver a package to his
work including a few of
his favorite things.

OCTOBER

During a disagreement, try this new communication technique: Listen carefully to your husband, then confirm back to him, in your own words, what you heard him saying. This is not to say you agree but are giving an earnest attempt to see things from his perspective. If you misunderstood him, it helps him to know he needs to change his wording. When you repeat it back, make sure not to interject your own feelings but convey you understand how he is feeling. For example, "What I hear you saying is that [paraphrase what you heard] and it makes you feel [describe how he feels]."

(Together) Change up the place you usually make love. Ideas: the office, the car, a different room of the house.

Give him a back scratch.

Buy new lingerie. Put it on and sashay up to him, saying, "I bought this for you to enjoy."

Plan a guys' night out for him.

NOVEMBER

(Usually, "Habit Reformations" are done together. This month, they are separate challenges.) Don't dump on him as soon as he walks in the door. Wait ten to fifteen minutes before you tell him about your day.

(Together) In most marriages, passionate kissing and long make-out sessions end shortly after marriage. Bring it back! Go into a locked room or closet and have a prolonged make-out session with no sexpectations.

(Extra credit: The next time you are out in public together, sneak into a corner or a bathroom for a quick "kiss & pet" session.)

Make sure to tell him when
he looks handsome.

The next time you're out in public together, blow him a kiss from across the room.

It's important for a man to know he can provide for his woman's sexual needs. While lovemaking, be bold about expressing—both verbally and through movement— that you're enjoying him.

DECEMBER

Do not belittle your husband.
Making him feel small will
only wedge you apart. If an
issue needs addressed, discuss it
only after you've had a chance
to calm down and without
degrading his character.

What are your husband's interests?
Search for a documentary
based on one of his interests
and watch it with him.

Massage his feet. If they're
gross and stinky, soak
and scrub them first.

Brag about him to your friends
when he's within earshot.

Text him, "I love it
when you _____."

Fill in the blank with a way
he physically touches you.

CONCLUSION

We hope you were able to find new ways to express love to each other and were brought closer together on this journey of marriage challenges. If you haven't already, consider participating in the full package of Marriage In Abundance, including date plans and couples' devotions. Find out how by visiting www.marriageinabundance.com. Stay tuned as there will be a second book with another year of fun and bonding activities coming soon!

APPENDIX

Proverbs 31:10-31 [Added thoughts are in brackets to make it culturally relatable.]

A wife of noble character who can find? She is worth far more than rubies. Her husband has full confidence in her and lacks nothing of value. She brings him good, not harm, all the days of her life. She selects wool and flax [provides for her family's needs] and works with eager hands. She is like the merchant ships, bringing her food from afar [providing for her family through sacrifice]. She gets up while it is still night; she provides food for her family and portions for her female servants [She provides, also, for those who help her]. She considers a field and buys it [She makes investment decisions with forethought]; out of her earnings she plants a vineyard [She plans and uses her money for future provision]. She sets about her work vigorously; her arms are strong for her tasks [She is not lazy; she keeps physically fit]. She sees that her trading [business deal] is profitable, and her lamp does not go out at night. In her hand she holds the distaff and grasps the spindle with her fingers [works hard]. She opens her arms to the poor and extends her hands to the needy. When it snows, she has no fear for her household; for all of them are clothed in scarlet. She makes coverings for her bed; she is clothed in fine linen and purple [She dresses respectably]. Her husband is respected at the city gate [in the community], where he takes his seat among the elders of the land. She makes linen garments and sells them, and supplies the merchants with sashes [works by providing for others]. She is clothed with strength and dignity; she can laugh at the days to come [She has joy and does not worry about the future (because, as stated earlier, she has done much to prepare for the future).]. She speaks with wisdom, and faithful instruction is on her tongue [She offers solid advice]. She watches over the affairs of her household and does not eat the bread of idleness [She is not lazy and does not waste her use of time]. Her children arise and call her blessed; her husband also, and he praises her: "Many women do noble things, but you surpass them all." Charm is deceptive, and beauty is fleeting [Her worth is not on her physical attributes]; but a woman who fears the Lord [desires to obey and honor God] is to be praised. Honor her for all that her hands have done, and let her works bring her praise at the city gate [within her community].

ABOUT THE AUTHOR

Mandy Shrock is the founder of Marriage In Abundance, a ministry aimed at deepening the bonds of married couples. In addition to writing materials for marriage improvement, she also wrote, *Life In Abundance,* devotions for anyone, no matter their stage in life. She is passionate about life, the Word of God, marriage, sci-fi and fantasy books, exercise, the outdoors, natural foods, and dogs. Powered by coffee, she lives with her husband, four children, and two dogs in northern Indiana.